JACOB

THE TIMELESS COLLECTION

OF OLD AGE JOKES

A JOKE BOOK FOR SENIORS
FOR BRAIN FITNESS AND GOOD MOOD

BOOST YOUR MEMORY FOR FREE!

**Stay young in mind and young at heart
with bonus rounds.**

Join our TRIVIA TRIBE **NOW!**

HAVE YOUR NAME IN THE CREDITS

Send us your favorite trivia question for a chance
to have it included in our next trivia book.
And yes, we'll have you in the credits!

Simply send us an email to:
funtriviawithjacob@gmail.com

DOWNLOAD OUR BOOKS FOR FREE!

You're one click away from our best-selling
books. Scan the QR code or follow the link below
to download all our trivia books for FREE.
Take advantage of this limited opportunity.

https://bit.ly/FunTriviaCollection

TABLE OF CONTENTS

Always find a reason

to laugh.

It may not add years

to your life

but will surely add life

to your years.

INTRODUCTION

Did you know that laughing has tons of health benefits?

Laughing your socks off brings about a good mood, relieves stress, keeps you young, and improves your overall sense of happiness. It really is the best medicine to avoid becoming old and grumpy.

Age blesses us with life experiences. Some are funny while others can be very challenging. Regardless, all life experiences can make funny anecdotes if you find the right angle. And this book is just that. It's a book filled with funny scenarios, classic jokes, and crazy puns that find joy and satire in things only people of old age would understand.

The Timeless Collection of Old Age Jokes will give you dozens of hours of clean jokes guaranteed to stir up smiles and belly laughs you can enjoy with friends and family.

He had tried many ways to quit smoking
but only one worked.

HOW OLD ARE YOU?

YOU ARE IN YOUR 60s

...when you hear your favorite songs in an elevator.

...when you're told to slow down by your doctor and not the police.

...when you eat supper at 5 p.m.

YOU ARE IN YOUR 70S

...when you have a hard time locating the keys in your pocket.

...when the oxygen masks drop from the ceiling when your birthday candles are lit.

YOU ARE IN YOUR 80S

...when you write a note to yourself reminding you not to take a sleeping pill and a laxative on the same night.

...when your staying power is for the cake.

YOU ARE IN YOUR 90S

...when kidnappers aren't very interested in you.

...when people no longer view you as a hypochondriac.

YOU ARE IN YOUR 100S

...when there is nothing left to learn the hard way.

...when you are too old to care.

...when you see expensive antiques and you remember one just like it that you threw away.

FUNNY STAGES OF LIFE

1972: Long hair
2010: Longing for hair

1972: The perfect high
2010: The perfect high yield mutual fund

1972: KEG
2010: EKG

1972: Acid rock
2010: Acid reflux

1972: Moving to California because it's cool
2010: Moving to California because it's warm

1972: Growing pot
2010: Growing pot belly

1972: Hoping for a BMW
2010: Hoping for a BM

1972: The Grateful Dead
2010: Dr. Kevorkian

1972: Rolling Stones
2010: Kidney Stones

1972: Being called into the principal's office
2010: Calling the principal's office

1972: Disco
2010: Costco

1972: Parents begging you to get your hair cut
2010: Children begging you to get their heads shaved

1972: Passing the drivers' test
2010: Passing the vision test

1972: Whatever
2010: Depends

"Of course, we're not gossiping about you."

BEHIND THE WHEEL

As a senior citizen was driving down the freeway, his cell phone rang. Picking up, he heard his wife, her voice high with anxiety, warn him, "Henry, I just saw on the news that there's a car driving the wrong way on Highway 880. Please be careful!"

"One?" replied Henry, "You've got to be kidding me. I see at least a hundred!"

THE PERKS OF BEING 60

One good thing about being 60: when you can't find your eyeglasses, they're almost always on your forehead.

. . .

Getting old has its advantages. I can no longer read the bathroom scale.

. . .

At my age, the only pole dancing I do is to hold on to the safety bar in the bathtub.

. . .

The older we get, the earlier it gets late.

. . .

There are four stages of old age: You forget names. Then you forget faces. Next, you forget to zip up. And finally, you forget to zip down.

When you're 20 and you drop something, you pick it up. When you're 80 and you drop something, you decide you don't need it anymore.

. . .

You know you're getting old when you can't walk past a bathroom without thinking, "I may as well pee while I'm here…"

. . .

The good thing about having a bad memory is that jokes can be funny more than once.

. . .

I called the incontinence hotline. They asked if I could hold.

. . .

I grew a beard thinking it would say "Distinguished Gentleman." Instead, turns out it says, "Senior Discount, please!"

Getting older has some benefits... Call it a "senior moment" and you can get away with pretty much anything!

...

When you relax on a park bench, boy scouts offer to help you cross your legs.

...

You know you're getting older when you use the word "thingy" all the time because you no longer can remember what things are called.

...

As you get older, three things happen. The first is your memory goes, and I can't remember the other two.

...

You know you're old when dining out means catching the early bird special.

One good thing about being 60 is you argue less. It's not so much that you're nicer, you just can't hear each other.

. . .

There are many advantages to being 60…Ask an 80-year-old.

. . .

One benefit of old age is that your secrets are safe with your friends — they can't remember them either!

. . .

With old age comes wisdom… and discounts!

. . .

Getting lucky means you found your car in the parking lot.

"I have no idea what the dress code allows,
but I bet it doesn't include jammies."

THE FAMOUS MAN

One day a famous man went to a nursing home to see all of his friends again and see how there were doing. When he got there everybody greeted him (because, of course, everybody knows him).

One man he noticed didn't come up to him or say anything to him, so later he walked up to the man and asked him "Do you know who I am?" and the old man replied, "No, but you can go to the front desk and they'll tell you."

AGE IS JUST A NUMBER

What goes up but never comes down? Your age!

· · ·

My teenage angst has lasted 30 years.

· · ·

I'm not old. I just need some WD-40!

· · ·

I've decided: Whatever age I am is the new 30.

· · ·

Why am I getting older and wider instead of older and wiser?

· · ·

Allow me to politely suggest this be the year you start lying about your age.

Old age isn't so bad when you consider the alternative.

. . .

Age is a relative thing. All your relatives keep reminding you how old you are.

. . .

Don't let your age get you down. After all, at your age, it's hard to get back up again.

. . .

They say that with old age comes wisdom. That must mean you're the wisest person in the world!

. . .

Age is an issue of mind over matter. If you don't mind, it doesn't matter!

. . .

Old people are just young people who have been alive for a very long time.

You're not getting older; you're just becoming a classic!

. . .

How old would you be if you didn't know how old you were?

. . .

Forget age. If you can still manage to blow out your birthday candles, everything is dandy.

. . .

If things get better with age, then we must be getting close to magnificent!

. . .

"If age is only in the mind, someone should tell that to my bones." — Melanie White

. . .

I believe in loyalty. So, when I got to a certain age, I decided to stick with it.

You know all of the answers, but nobody asks you the questions anymore.

. . .

Being older brings its own pleasures. Nothing tops eating chocolate candy while the taste of toothpaste is still fresh in your mouth.

. . .

You talk about "good grass" and mean someone's lawn.

"Well, they seemed nice."

SOMEBODY GET THE DOOR

One evening, two old men from a retirement home were sitting on the front porch of the retirement home. One man said to the other old man, "You know, Albert, if you think about it, we are not that old. I mean, my memory is still very good."

As the man said this, he knocked on the wooden chair beside him. "Actually, as sharp as ever." After a couple of minutes of silence, the first man started to talk again, "So, is anyone going to get the door, or do I have to do it?"

LOVE YOUR HUMOR

That bizarre moment when you pick up your car from the garage and you realize that the breaks are still not working, but they made your horn louder.

. . .

When I see lovers' names carved in a tree, I don't think it's sweet. I just think it's surprising how many people bring a knife on a date.

. . .

I had a dream where an evil queen forced me to eat a gigantic marshmallow. When I woke up, my pillow was gone.

. . .

When you put a bed in your bedroom – you have less bedroom.

Years ago, I threw away a boomerang really hard. I've lived in constant fear since.

...

I can't believe I forgot to go to the gym today. That's 7 years in a row now.

...

I received another letter from some lawyer yesterday. It had "Final Notice" written on the envelope. Good. They won't be bothering me anymore.

...

We have a strange custom in our office. The food has names there. Yesterday, for example, I got a sandwich out of the fridge and its name was "Michael".

...

Why haven't you ever seen any elephants hiding up trees? Because they're really, really good at it.

"Siri, why am I still single?!"
Siri activates the front camera.

...

My doctor told me I must stop playing football.

"What?! Is he sure? Did he examine you properly?"

"Not really. But he did see me playing."

...

I don't recommend getting older cause I don't think it is good for your health.

...

If you don't learn to laugh at trouble, you won't have anything to laugh at when you are old.

...

You know you are getting old when everything either dries up or leaks.

If God wanted me to touch my toes, he would have put them on my knees.

. . .

If all is not lost, where is it?

. . .

It is easier to get older than it is to get wiser.

. . .

These days about half the stuff in my shopping cart says, "For fast relief."

. . .

These days, I spend a lot of time thinking about the hereafter ... I go somewhere to get something, and then wonder what I'm here after.

"Can I buy a vowel?"

LOST

A retired woman calls 911 on her cellphone to report that her car has been broken into. She is hysterical as she explains her situation to the dispatcher: "They've stolen the stereo, the steering wheel, the brake pedal and even the accelerator!" she cries.

The dispatcher replies reassuringly, "Don't worry, ma'am. An officer is on his way."

A few minutes later, the dispatched officer calls in. "Disregard," he says. "She got into the back seat by mistake."

LAUGH OUT LOUD!

I'm going to open a nightclub for senior citizens, The Soft Rock Cafe.

. . .

Don't you wish that you were as old as the first time you thought you were old?

. . .

You're so old you get status updates on your friends from the obituary section.

. . .

You truly deserve to be treasured. After all, fossils from your era are hard to find.

. . .

When you were born, the Dead Sea was only sick.

I've got a great tip for you in your old age. Instead of calling the bathroom "the John," call it "the Jim." That way you can tell people, "I go to the Jim the first thing every morning!"

. . .

At my age, flowers scare me.

. . .

I always wanted to marry an Archeologist. The older I would get, the more interested she would become!

. . .

As I get older and remember all the people I've lost along the way. I think to myself maybe a career as a tour guide wasn't for me.

. . .

Why do Retirees smile all the time? Because they can't hear a word you're saying!

We'll be friends 'til we're old and senile... and then we'll be new friends!

...

I swear, if my memory was any worse, I could plan my own surprise party!

...

You save a ton of money on shampoo, not because of your senior discount, but because you now have too little hair to bother with it.

...

You still miss your high school car, but you can't remember your classmates.

...

I have reached an age when, if someone tells me to wear socks, I don't have to.

Wouldn't it be great if we could put ourselves in the dryer for 10 minutes and come out wrinkle-free?

. . .

What's the advantage of having kids at 49? You can both be in diapers at the same time?

. . .

The easiest way to find something that's lost around the house is to buy a replacement.

. . .

"At my age I've heard it all; I've seen it all, and I've done it all. I just can't remember it all. "

— Author Unknown

"He's trying to feel
which way the wind is blowing."

TAKE THE DOCTOR'S ADVICE

Morris, an 82-year-old man, went to the doctor to get a physical exam. A few days later the doctor saw Morris walking down the street with a gorgeous young woman on his arm. A couple of days later the doctor spoke to Morris and said, "You're really doing great, aren't you?" Morris replied, "Just doing what you said, Doc. Get a hot mamma and be cheerful.' The doctor said, "I didn't say that. I said you've got a heart murmur. Be careful."

DOCTOR'S APPOINTMENT

Dentist: You need a crown.

Patient: Finally, someone who understands me.

...

Doctor: You're obese.

Patient: For that, I definitely want a second opinion.

Doctor: You're quite ugly, too.

...

Patient: Oh Doctor, I'm starting to forget things.

Doctor: Since when have you had this condition?

Patient: What condition?

...

Mr. Smith: Doctor, do you remember this strengthening solution you prescribed me yesterday?

Doctor: Yes, what's the matter?

Mr. Smith: I would like to use it but I can't open the bottle!

. . .

Patient: Doctor help me please, every time I drink a cup of coffee, I get this intense stinging in my eye.

Doctor: I suggest you remove the spoon before drinking.

. . .

Doctor: I've found a great new drug that can help you with your sleeping problem.

Patient: Great, how often do I have to take it?

Doctor: Every two hours.

. . .

Nurse to a doctor: Doctor, here's your list of heart, liver, and kidney donors. I already sorted them alphabetically.

A doctor told his patient, "There's good news and bad news. The bad news is, you have partial short-term memory loss." The patient said, "Oh no, Doctor. What's the bad news?"

. . .

ER DOCTOR: So, what brings you here?

PATIENT: An ambulance! What do you think?!

. . .

A patient at my daughter's medical clinic filled out a form. After Name and Address, the next question was "Nearest Relative." She wrote "Walking distance."

. . .

The doctor will be in shortly to type on the computer and update your chart. If he has time, he will ask how you're feeling and take a look at your rash.

Doctor: Excellent job. Seriously well organ-ized.

. . .

I've done a battery of tests on you and the only suggestion that I can make is that you need a new battery.

. . .

Patient: Doctor, my wife drunk a liter of petrol. What can I do?

Doctor: Ask her to run 60Km. Then it'll be alright.

. . .

Patient: Can you diagnose my illness?

Doctor: Your eyesight seems to be poor.

Patient: How did you come to that conclusion?

Doctor: Even you couldn't read the front board sign. This is a Veterinary hospital.

"I can buy only things that are vegan, organic, natural, local, eco aware and comforting."

WRONG INSERT

Two elderly women were eating breakfast in a restaurant one morning. Ethel noticed something funny about Mabel's ear and she said, "Mabel, did you know you've got a suppository in your left ear?" Mabel answered, "I have a suppository?" She pulled it out and stared at it. Then she said, "Ethel, I'm glad you saw this thing. Now I think I know where my hearing aid is."

FUNNIEST CONVERSATIONS EVER HEARD

A guest is ordering at a restaurant, "Do you think you could bring me what that gentleman over there is having?"

The waiter looks at him sternly, "No sir, I'm very sure he intends to eat it himself."

• • •

The husband looks at his wife in surprise, "Wow darling, you look all different and nice today! Is that a new hairdo?"

The wife hisses from behind him, "I'm over here, Arnold!"

• • •

"Waiter, the steak smells very strongly of liquor!"

The waiter backs up 3 steps and asks, "How's that now?"

A chubbier woman: Mirror, Mirror on the wall, who's the fairest of them all?

Mirror: Kindly move aside. I can't see anything.

. . .

"OK, that's it, I'm leaving you! You're SO childish!"

"Well, good luck with that - because the floor is lava!"

. . .

Employee: Can I have a raise?

Boss: Nope.

Employee: Ok, let me rephrase it. Give me a raise or I will tell my 75 co-workers that I got one.

. . .

"Darling, I think the new dryer is shrinking my clothes."

"No, sweetie, that was the fridge."

Guest at a restaurant: "I refuse to eat this roast beef. Please call the manager! "

Waiter: "That's no use. He won't eat it either."

• • •

Daddy somebody's at the door. He's collecting for the district's new indoor swimming pool.

Ok, give him a bucket of water then.

• • •

"I want to win 10 million in the lottery, just like my dad did!"

"OMG, your dad won 10 million in the lottery?!"

"No, but he always wanted to."

• • •

An old teacher asked her student, "If I say, 'I am beautiful,' which tense is that?"

The student replied, "It is obviously past."

When my grandson asked me how old I was, I teasingly replied, "I'm not sure."

"Look in your underwear, Grandpa," he advised "Mine says I'm 4 to 6."

. . .

"And what do you think is the best thing about being 104?" the reporter asked.

She simply replied, "No peer pressure."

. . .

Two old women were sitting side-by-side in their rocking chairs when one said to the other, "I'm getting so old all my friends in Heaven are going to think I didn't make it."

"This is one of his early pieces."

MISSING CARAMEL

Two older gentlemen, Fred and Sam, went to see a movie. Merely minutes into the movie, Sam heard Fred rustling around. It appeared that he was reaching under all of the seats. "What on earth are you doing, Fred?" asked Sam. Fred indignantly responded, "I had a caramel in my mouth and it dropped out. I'm trying to find it!" Annoyed, Sam told him not to worry about it — they could get him another caramel later since that one was ruined by now. "But I've got to," said Fred, exasperated. "My teeth are in it!"

ANATOMY OF A SENIOR CITIZEN

How are stars like false teeth? They both come out at night!

...

If my body were a car, I would trade it for a newer model...every time I cough sneeze, or sputter my radiant leaks and my exhaust backfires.

...

I'm not hard of hearing. I've just heard enough.

...

What was the radioactive older adult's superpower? Gramma rays.

...

Congratulations on being able to cough, fart, sneeze, and pee at the same time!

You know you're old when your back goes out more than you do.

. . .

Don't stress about your eyesight failing as you get older. It's nature's way of keeping you from shock when you go by a mirror.

. . .

Did you know that there's a prize for getting older? Yep – you get atrophy.

. . .

You've reached the age when everything is now beginning to click. Your knees, your hips, your elbows.

. . .

At this age, when you roll a joint it's probably just your ankle.

I'm at the age where I have to make a noise when I bend over. It's the law.

. . .

You know you're getting older when an "all-nighter" means not getting up to pee.

. . .

Your joints snap, crackle, and pop more than your Rice Krispies.

. . .

Your ankles start sagging over the top of your anklets.

. . .

It's great to have gray hair. Ask anyone who's bald.

. . .

Don't think about wrinkles. It's called 60's dimples.

60 is the peak. After 60, the body is weak.

· · ·

I look 40 and act 20; that made me 60.

· · ·

Your knees buckle, and your belt won't.

· · ·

You have two parts of the brain, "left" and "right". On the left side, there's nothing right and on the right side, there's nothing left.

· · ·

Know how to prevent sagging? Just eat till the wrinkles fill out.

· · ·

Your memory is shorter and your complaining lasts longer.

"Tomorrow I'll teach you how to land."

TERMS OF ENDEARMENT

An elderly gent was invited to his old friend's home for dinner one evening. He was impressed by the way his buddy preceded every request to his wife with endearing terms - Honey, My Love, Darling, Sweetheart, Pumpkin, etc.

The couple had been married almost 70 years, and clearly, they were still very much in love. While the wife was in the kitchen, the man leaned over and said to his host, "I think it's wonderful that, after all these years, you still call your wife those loving pet names."

The old many hung his head. "I have to tell you the truth," he said, "I forgot her name about 10 years ago."

FUNNY FAMILY MOMENTS

Boy comes up to his father, all angry, "Dad, you remember how you told me to put a potato in my swimming trunks? How you said it would impress the girls?"

Father looks up, smiling, "Yeah, did it work?"

The boy screams, "You could have mentioned that the potato goes in the front!"

. . .

I lent my girlfriend a lot of money for cosmetic surgery a while ago. I've been trying to get it back now for weeks.

Problem is, I've no idea what she looks like now.

. . .

Wow, honey, I never thought our son would go that far!

Yeah, the catapult is really amazing. Go get our daughter!

A boy and his father go together for a boys' day out at the zoo.

"Daddy, I don't like how that gorilla's looking at me from behind that glass, she's quite scary!" says the boy.

"Shush, Jason!!!! This is still only the ticket office!"

. . .

"Daddy, what is an alcoholic?"

"Do you see those 4 trees, son? An alcoholic would see 8 trees."

"Um, Dad – there are only 2 trees."

. . .

Wife calls her mother: "Today I fought so much with my husband. I am coming to live with you again.

Mother: "No. He should pay for his mistake. I am coming to live with you."

I asked my daughter if she'd seen my newspaper. She told me that newspapers are old school. She said that people use tablets nowadays and handed me her iPad. The fly didn't stand a chance.

. . .

My wife is always stealing my t-shirts and sweaters... But if I take one of her dresses, suddenly "we need to talk".

. . .

I had an argument with my husband, and he made me really mad. So, I went to take a shower, being angry with him every single second. And suddenly I realized that I completely forgot the reason for my anger.

. . .

Grandma was standing at the foot of the stair and asked me, "One thing I can't remember, was I going up or down?"

When my grandson Billy and I entered our vacation cabin, we kept the lights off until we were inside to keep from attracting pesky insects. Still, a few fireflies followed us in. Noticing them before I did, Billy whispered, "It's no use Grandpa. Now the mosquitoes are coming after us with flashlights."

. . .

My sister rocks. She came home after a birthday party, and when Mom asked, "Did you drink?" she answered, "A wlass of gine."

. . .

Dad kept jumping in with off-topic comments and asking for things to be repeated. I told him he needed to get a hearing aid.

Looking at me as if I were crazy, he said, "What would I do with a hand grenade?"

"Give you a wakeup call for New Year's Eve?
Okay, but you have to give me one, too."

DRIVER'S LICENSE

I've sure gotten old! I've had two bypass surgeries, a hip replacement, new knees, fought prostate cancer and diabetes. I'm half blind, can't hear anything quieter than a jet engine, take 40 different medications that make me dizzy, winded, and subject to blackouts. Have bouts with dementia. Have poor circulation; hardly feel my hands and feet anymore. Can't remember if I'm 85 or 92. Have lost all my friends. But, thank God, I still have my driver's license!

OLDIES AND THEIR HOBBIES

You no longer need a spoon to stir the creamer in your coffee. You just pour the milk in and let your shaky hand do the job.

...

How do you know your old? People call at 9 p.m. and ask, "Did I wake you?"

...

The old man moved to Hawaii to live the life of a dentured surfing dude.

...

When you're young you make a lot of noise just having fun. When you're old, you make even more noise just bending over.

...

The old folk's home was very secure. Each door was guarded by a century.

Only old people watch the Grammy Awards.

. . .

Remember, you don't have to rewind Netflix videos when you're done watching a movie.

. . .

You're so old you walked into an antique store and they tried to sell you.

. . .

This year, may you always get up off the couch in two tries or less.

. . .

The only reason I'm jogging is so that I can hear my heavy breathing again.

. . .

By the time a man is wise enough to watch his step, he's too old to go anywhere.

Your recliner has more controls than your motor vehicle.

. . .

You know you're getting old when you start watching golf on TV and enjoying it.

. . .

Your idea of a night out is sitting on the patio.

. . .

I've reached the age when looking in the mirror is like checking the news. I know there'll be some new developments I won't like.

. . .

When is a retiree's bedtime? Three hours after he falls asleep on the couch.

. . .

If the music's too loud you're too old.

At 60, two of the most important things in life are bowel movements and nose hair.

. . .

A short nap once in a while can prevent old age especially while driving.

. . .

I started belly dancing today. It was so easy, no effort at all. I just gave it a little shake and my belly danced all on its own.

. . .

You have that "morning after" feeling when you wake up, but you didn't party the night before.

. . .

Now that I'm 60, every morning I look in the mirror and say, "I don't know who you are, stranger, but I'm gonna shave you anyway." —Milton Friedman

No offense, but I just can't buy food with a shelf
life longer than my life expectancy.

THE PRESIDENT

A grandmother noticed that her grandson was spending way too much time playing computer games. In an effort to motivate the boy into focusing more attention on his schoolwork, the grandmother said to her grandson, 'When Abe Lincoln was your age, he was studying books by the light of the fireplace.'

The grandson replied, 'Grandma, when Lincoln was your age, he was The President of The United States!!!'

'CAUSE IT'S PUN-NIER!

I got my girlfriend a 'Get better soon' card.

She's not ill or anything, but she could definitely get better.

. . .

I fear my stuttering brother may never finish his prison sentence.

. . .

A doctor got angry. He lost all his patients.

. . .

The longest I've ever gone without a pun was 7 days. Pretty weak.

. . .

This gravity joke is getting a bit old, but I fall for it every time.

Why did the balloon go near the needle? He wanted to be a pop star.

. . .

I was hoping to steal some leftovers from the party but I guess my plans were foiled.

. . .

You're becoming a vegetarian? I think that's a big missed steak.

. . .

What would you call an obese psychic? A four-chin teller.

. . .

Which country's capital is the fastest growing?

Answer: Ireland's. Every year it's Dublin.

. . .

Why was the chef arrested? He was beating eggs every day.

Jokes about unemployed people are not funny. They just don't work.

. . .

A boy ate some coins for fun and his parents took him to the hospital. One hour later the parents asked the nurse how it was going. Apparently, "no change yet."

. . .

I'm getting really claustrophobic in elevators. I've had to start taking steps to avoid it.

. . .

I dig, you dig, she digs, we dig, you dig…the poem may not be beautiful, but it's certainly very deep.

. . .

I know that I'm fat but I'd be really rich in Britain. There they measure their wealth in pounds.

I'd love to know how the Earth rotates. It would totally make my day.

. . .

I owe a lot to the sidewalks. They've been keeping me off the streets for years.

. . .

A man sued an airline company after it lost his luggage. Sadly, he lost his case.

. . .

Shouldn't pregnant women be called bodybuilders?

. . .

If you spent your day in a well, can you say your day was well-spent?

. . .

I once worked in a bank, but then I lost interest.

"We'll never guess her password."

WHAT'S FOR DESSERT?

An elderly couple was watching television one evening. The wife said, "I am going to get a dish of ice cream now." Kindly, the husband offered to get the ice cream for his wife. "I'll write it down so you don't forget," she said.

"I won't forget," the old gent said. "But I want chocolate syrup and nuts on it. So, I'll write it down," she replied.

"I will get you the ice cream. Don't you worry," replied the gentleman.

A few minutes later, the old man returned with bacon and eggs. His wife said, "See, I should have written it down because you forgot the toast."

GOLDEN FOOD FOR GOLDEN YEARS

Pastry chefs know that old age crepes up on you.

...

You may be old, but I don't carrot all!

...

The old baker understands aging, she's an old tarte!

...

You know what the young chicken said the old, "You're no spring chicken!"

...

Age got muffin on you!

...

Things that age well: Wine. Cheese. You.

Age gets better with wine.

. . .

As you get older, don't bother eating healthy food; go for packaged junk. You're going to need all the preservatives you can get.

. . .

You and wine are the perfect pair. Wine improves with age, and you improve with wine.

. . .

I'm not saying you're old, but if you were whiskey, you'd be expensive. Really expensive.

. . .

In wine years, you are extra fine.

. . .

The older you get, the better you get. Unless you're a banana.

He is so old that if he orders a three-minute egg, they will demand money in advance.

. . .

What's the difference between people and tin foil? Tin foil doesn't wrinkle as it oldens.

. . .

Instead of adding blueberries to your cornflakes, you just sprinkle them with your morning medications.

. . .

The cardiologist's diet: If it tastes good spit it out.

– Anonymous

. . .

Going for a walk because I want to stay healthy. Taking along a box of M&M's because let's be honest here.

Diet Day #1 - I removed all the fattening food from my house. It was delicious.

· · ·

Just asked my wife what she's "burning up for dinner" and it turned out to be all of my personal belongings.

· · ·

The dinner I was cooking for my family was going to be a surprise but the fire trucks ruined it.

· · ·

I entered what I ate today into my new fitness app and it just sent an ambulance to my house.

· · ·

I am on a seafood diet. Every time I see food, I eat it.

"I could swear the invitation said '7am'."

THE MEDICAL RESULT

The man told his doctor that he wasn't able to do all the things around the house that he used to do.

When the examination was complete, he said, "Now, Doc, I can take it. Tell me in plain English what is wrong with me." "Well, in plain English," the doctor replied, "you're just lazy." "OK," said the man. "Now give me the medical term so I can tell my wife."

FUNNIEST ONE-LINERS EVER HEARD

I stole my friend's wheelchair. Guess who comes crawling back to me?!

. . .

Talk is cheap, yeah? Have you ever talked to a lawyer?!

. . .

If we shouldn't eat at night, why do they put a light in the fridge?

. . .

I hate it when I run out of toilet paper and I have to make the trip to the grocery store in really small steps.

. . .

I have clean conscience. I haven't used it once till now.

Chocolate is the best investment. You buy 100 g – you gain 2 kg!

. . .

I used to breed rabbits. Then I realized they can handle it themselves.

. . .

My dog is an awesome fashion adviser. Every time I ask him what I look like in my clothes, he says "WOW!"

. . .

Do not go to the bathroom in a dream. It's a trap!

. . .

I heard women love a man in uniform. Can't wait to start working at McDonalds.

. . .

My IQ test results came back. They were negative.

My father is allergic to cotton. He has pills he can take, but he can't get them out of the bottle.

. . .

Money talks. Mine always says goodbye.

. . .

Don't spell part backward. It's a trap.

. . .

I find it ironic that the colors red, white, and blue stand for freedom until they are flashing behind you.

. . .

If money doesn't grow on trees, how come banks have branches?

. . .

When everything is coming your way — you're in the wrong lane.

"My father drank so heavily, when he blew on the birthday cake, he lit the candles."

— Les Dawson

• • •

My wife told me to stop impersonating a flamingo. I had to put my foot down.

• • •

My wife just found out I replaced our bed with a trampoline; she hit the roof.

• • •

I heard a great joke about amnesia but I forgot it.

• • •

At every party, there are two kinds of people: those who want to go home and those who don't. The trouble is, they are usually married to each other.

Feeling pretty proud of myself. The puzzle I bought said 3-5 years, but I finished it in 18 months.

...

Time may be a great healer but it's also a lousy beautician.

...

Women usually claim childbirth is the most painful experience of their lives. Until they start stepping on Legos approximately three years later.

...

Sorry I just saw your text from last night, are you guys still at the restaurant?

...

I nearly drowned yesterday. It was a breathtaking experience.

After 40 years, my grandma has finally gotten my grandpa to stop biting his nails. She's hidden his teeth.

. . .

My grandpa started walking five miles a day when he was 60. Now he's 97 years old, and we have no idea where he is.

. . .

My dear old grandmother always used to say the way to a man's heart was through his stomach. That's why she lost her job as a cardiac surgeon.

. . .

My grandpa said he was built upside down. His nose runs and his feet smell.

I think you'll be interested in the next patient. He's 92 years old and accompanied by his parents.

TEST OF FRIENDSHIP

Two elderly ladies had been friends for many decades. Over the years they had shared all kinds of activities and adventures. Lately, their activities had been limited to meeting a few times a week to play cards. One day they were playing cards when one looked at the other and said, "Now don't get mad at me. I know we've been friends for a long time but I just can't think of your name! I've thought and thought, but I can't remember it. Please tell me what your name is." Her friend glared at her. For at least three minutes...she just stared and glared at her. Finally, she said, "How soon do you need to know?"

LIFE BEGINS AT 60

The seven ages of man: spills, drills, thrills, bills, ills, pills, and wills.

. . .

Young at heart, old everywhere else.

. . .

Being an adult is just walking around wondering what you're forgetting.

. . .

Work hard and save your money and when you are old you will be able to buy the things only the young can enjoy.

. . .

The older you get, the more you need to keep a fire extinguisher close to the cake.

There are so many medication bottles in your bathroom cabinet that you no longer have room for cosmetics and toothpaste.

. . .

This is not what adulthood looked like in the brochure.

. . .

How can you say that you're getting old? You go to an antique auction and three people bid on you!

. . .

I've reached an age where my train of thought often leaves the station without me.

. . .

You start getting carded again, but now cashiers want to see your senior card to make sure you're old enough to qualify for the discount.

Just remember, it's better to pay full price than to admit you're a senior citizen.

. . .

You finally have to admit that your "character lines" are really just wrinkles.

. . .

You start wondering who that old woman/man is looking at your window and realize you're standing in front of the mirror.

. . .

You used to make fun of adult diaper commercials, and now you're clipping coupons for them "just in case."

. . .

60th birthday thrills: more pills, more chills, and more bills. —Greg Tamblyn

You know you're getting older when you have a party and the neighbors don't even realize it.

. . .

Sometimes I wish I had the wisdom of a 90-year-old, the body of a 20-year-old, and the energy of a 3-year-old.

. . .

I am not old. I prefer the term "youthfully challenged."

. . .

Old age is like a plane flying through a storm. Once you are aboard there is nothing you can do about it.

. . .

If you lose something in an old-age home, don't stop until you've searched every nook and granny.

Feel free to get a second opinion. I can give you the number of my mom.

ONE YEAR

An old man goes to the doctor for a checkup. After extensive tests the doctor tells him "I'm afraid I have some bad news for you. You only have six months to live." The man is dumbstruck. After a while he replies "That's terrible doctor. But I must admit to you that I can't afford to pay your bill." "Ok" says the doctor, "I'll give you a year to live."

FLAUNT YOUR HAIR

With old age comes great wisdom and hairs in weird places that need to be plucked.

• • •

You know you're getting old when the little old gray-haired lady you helped across the street is your wife.

• • •

Don't worry, they are not gray hairs, they are wisdom-highlights. You just happen to be extremely wise.

• • •

Those aren't grey hair you see. They're strands of birthday glitter growing out of your head.

• • •

A little gray hair is a small price to pay for so much wisdom.

If gray hair is a sign of wisdom, then you're a genius!

• • •

Gray hair makes you look distinguished. It distinguishes you from younger people.

• • •

No, they aren't gray hairs. I am just so fabulous that even my hair sparkles.

• • •

They are not gray hairs! They are all-natural non-chemical highlights.

• • •

Got it! My last gray hair.

• • •

The day I found my first gray hair, I thought I'd dye!

Gray hair is hereditary. We get it from our children.

. . .

Thought I found a gray hair. It's a cat's hair anyway!

. . .

Let's be honest. Gray hair is God's way of keeping us in business.

. . .

They're not gray hair. I am just growing tinsel.

. . .

My wife said she wanted to see 50 Shades of Grey. So, I took a photo of her hair!

. . .

I just got my first grey hair. This is the last time I let grandma cook dinner for me.

Mommy, why are some of your hairs turning grey?

It is because of you, dear. Every bad action of yours will turn one of my hairs grey!

Now I know why grandmother has only grey hairs on her head.

· · ·

I don't need a hair stylist; my pillow gives me a new hairstyle every morning.

· · ·

That awkward moment when someone asks if your hair is wet, but it's just that dirty.

Fill out these 'new patient' forms,
but leave 'age' blank, as you may age
a year before you're done.

THREE OLD LADIES

Three older ladies were discussing the travails of getting older. One said, "Sometimes I catch myself with a jar of mayonnaise in my hand in front of the refrigerator and can't remember whether I need to put it away, or start making a sandwich."

The second lady chimed in, "Yes, sometimes I find myself on the landing of the stairs and can't remember whether I was on my way up or on my way down."

The third one responded, "Well, I'm glad I don't have that problem; knock on wood" as she wrapped her knuckles on the table. Then said, "That must be the door, I'll get it!"

IT'S YOUR BIRTHDAY!

Congrats on reaching the wonderful years! You wonder where your keys are, wonder what day it is, wonder where your car is parked.

. . .

At least you're not as old as you will be next year!

. . .

Don't worry about getting older. You're still going to do silly stuff, only slower.

. . .

It's your birthday – time to let your hair down! Oh, wait. I forgot; you don't have any.

. . .

You're so old, I heard your social security number is 3.

Your birthday is becoming a serious fire hazard with all those candles.

. . .

I wanted to give you a funny card, but I was concerned that at your age you might pee yourself.

. . .

So...how old are we pretending to be this year?

. . .

One year closer to being back in diapers.

. . .

It's your birthday – smile while you still have teeth!

. . .

I'm going to take you out to dinner for your birthday – do you think you can get us all the senior discount?!?

"You know you're getting old when you get that one candle on the cake. It's like, 'See if you can blow this out." —Jerry Seinfeld

...

We're going to try and get all the candles on your cake lit before the first ones burn down.

...

The tragedy of getting old: So many candles... so little cake!

...

Birthdays are good for you. The more you have, the longer you live!

...

My young grandson called the other day to wish me Happy Birthday. He asked me how old I was, and I told him, 62. My grandson was quiet for a moment, and then he asked, "Did you start at 1?"

Your brand-new lighter runs out of fluid before you can light all five-dozen candles on your cake.

...

Another year closer to hearing aids, walkers, and velcro shoes!

...

If it's your birthday today, you should congratulate yourself. Especially if you're still able to remember it.

...

"You know you're getting old when the candles cost more than the cake." — Bob Hope

...

"Your lifestyle really doesn't require
a Guardian Angel."

A HUNDRED YEARS

When my grandfather was in his eighties, he decided to move to Israel and went to a doctor to get all his charts and so on. He asked him how he was doing and he listed his complaints: "This hurts, that's stiff, I'm getting more and more tired and slower..."

"You have to expect things to start deteriorating. After all who wants to live to be 100?"

"Someone who's in their eighties," she replied.

YOU KNOW YOU ARE OLD

You know you are old when you look down at your watch three consecutive times and still don't know what time it is.

· · ·

You know you are old when you stop searching for the meaning of life to focus on searching for your car keys.

· · ·

You know you are old when you buy pills to improve your memory but forget where you put them.

· · ·

You know you are old when your brain cells are down to a manageable size.

You know you are old when you're young at heart, but you can't say the same for your other organs.

. . .

You know you are old when Happy Hour is a nap.

. . .

You know you are old when you want to take back all those times you didn't nap when you were younger.

. . .

You know you are old when getting lucky means a short wait in the doctor's office.

. . .

You know you are old when your back is hairier than your head.

You know you are old when a kid you once babysat is now your lawyer.

• • •

You know you are old when someone offers you a seat on the bus. And you don't refuse.

• • •

You know you are old when you speed because you don't want to forget where you're going.

• • •

You know you are old when your day starts backward. You wake up tired and go to bed wide awake!

• • •

You know you're old when you put your pajamas and slippers on at the time when you go out!

You know you're old when you sit on a rocking chair and can't get it going.

. . .

You know you're old when it takes longer to rest than it did to get tired.

. . .

You know you're old when you confuse having a clear conscience with a bad memory.

. . .

You know you're old when your address book has mostly names that start with Dr.

. . .

You know you're old when the pharmacist has become your new best friend.

. . .

You know you're old when you go out your energy runs out before your money does.

You know you're old when you're the one calling the police because those kids next door are having a loud party.

. . .

"You know you're getting older when you're told to slow down by your doctor, instead of by the police." — Joan Rivers

. . .

You know you're old when you and your teeth don't sleep together.

. . .

You know you're old when your idea of weight lifting is standing up.

. . .

You know you're old when you give up all your bad habits and still don't feel good.

You know you're old when you try to straighten out the wrinkles in your socks and discover you aren't wearing any.

. . .

You know you're old when you sink your teeth into a steak - and they stay there.

. . .

You know you're old when it takes twice as long - to look half as good.

. . .

You know you're old when a dripping faucet causes an uncontrollable bladder urge.

"Do you solemnly swear to listen to my advice?"

THE SECRET TO LONG LIFE

A man, celebrating his 100th birthday, was being interviewed by the local newspaper reporter. "And what do you attribute your longevity to?" asked the reporter. The centenarian answered, "I make sure I get up every morning". The puzzled reporter asked, "And just how do you do that?" The man answered, "I drink six glasses of water before I go to bed."

WITTY QUOTES

"I can't wait to tell my kids I was born before the Internet." —Unknown

"Everything slows down with age; except the time it takes cake and ice cream to reach your hips." —John Wagner

"I've learned that life is like a roll of toilet paper. The closer it gets to the end, the faster it goes." —Andy Rooney

"By the time a man is wise enough to watch his step, he's too old to go anywhere." —Billy Crystal

"Age is a very high price to pay for maturity." —Tom Stoppard

"At my age 'getting lucky' means walking into a room and remembering what I came in for." — Unknown

"Age is something that doesn't matter unless you are a cheese." — Luis Buñuel

"I don't let my age define me but the side effects are getting harder to ignore." — Unknown

"Forty is the old age of youth; fifty is the youth of old age." — Victor Hugo

"Don't let ageing get you down. It's too hard to get back up." — John Wagner

"Age is just a number that changes depending on who's asking." — Unknown

"Old age is always ten years older than me."
—Unknown

"Today is the oldest you've ever been and the youngest you'll ever be again." —Unknown

"Old age is not so bad when you consider the alternative. " —Maurice Chevalier

"Growing old is mandatory but growing up is optional." —Walt Disney

"As you get older, three things happen: The first is your memory goes, and I can't remember the other two." —Norman Wisdom

"The secret of staying young is to live honestly, eat slowly, and lie about your age." —Lucille Ball

"An archaeologist is the best husband a woman can have. The older she gets the more interested he is in her. " — Agatha Christie

"When you are dissatisfied and would like to go back to youth, think of algebra." — Will Rogers

"My grandmother was a very tough woman. She buried three husbands and two of them were just napping." — Rita Rudner

"Whatever you may look like, marry a man your own age -- as your beauty fades, so will his eyesight. " — Phyllis Diller

"True terror is to wake up one morning and discover that your high school class is running the country. " — Kurt Vonnegut

"I'm so old they've canceled my blood type." —Bob Hope

"Another tissue sample. I have to sneeze."

MEAL SHARING

A young man saw an elderly couple sitting down to lunch at McDonald's. He noticed that they had ordered one meal, and an extra drink cup. As he watched, the gentleman carefully divided the food in half. The old man then began to eat, and his wife sat watching, with her hands folded in her lap. The young man decided to ask if they would allow him to purchase another meal for them so that they didn't have to split theirs. The old gentleman said, "Oh, no. We've been married 50 years, and everything has always been and will always be shared 50/50." The young man then asked the wife if she was going to eat, and she replied, "Not yet. It's his turn with the teeth."

HILARIOUS SENIOR MOMENTS

I just saw a grandpa help a youngster who was staring into his phone, to cross the street.

. . .

Three old guys are out walking. The first one says, "Windy, isn't it?" The second one says, "No, it's Thursday!" The third one says, "I am thirsty too. Let's go get a beer."

. . .

One of the shortest wills ever written: "Being of sound mind, I spent all the money."

. . .

A senior is sitting at a bar when a young woman walks in and sits down a few seats over. The senior man gets up, shuffles over to her, leans in, and asks, "So... do I come here often?"

Speaking to her 93-year-old grandfather, a young woman asked, "Grandpa, what were your good old days?" Grandpa's reply? "When I wasn't good, and I wasn't old."

. . .

An older gentleman shuffled slowly into an ice cream parlor and pulled himself slowly, rather painfully looking, onto a stool. After catching his breath, he ordered a banana split supreme. The waitress smiled kindly at him, asking, "Crushed nuts?" The older gentleman replied, "No... arthritis."

. . .

My grandfather tried to warn them about the Titanic. He screamed and shouted about the iceberg and how the ship was going to sink, but all they did was throw him out of the theater.

. . .

Somewhere an elderly lady reads a book on how to use the internet, while a young boy googles "how to read a book".

Grandma's been staring through the window ever since it started to snow. If it gets any worse, I'll have to let her in.

...

A fellow tells his ma that there are two holes in his trousers — and then tells her that's where he puts his feet through. Cincinnati Enquirer, Nov. 1, 1896.

...

I want to die peacefully in my sleep, like my grandfather... Not screaming and yelling like the passengers in his car.

...

A retired man volunteers to entertain patients in assisted living homes. After telling jokes and singing songs at patients' bedsides, he said farewell and, "I hope you get better."

One elderly gentleman replied, "I hope you get better, too."

Old Man 1: If Abraham Lincoln were alive today, what would he be famous for?

Old Man 2: Old age.

...

An old man went down to my local supermarket and he said: "I want to make a complaint. This vinegar's got lumps in it". The cashier said: "Those are pickled onions."

...

Patient: "Doctor, please help me, I think I can see in the future."

Doctor: "When did it start?"

Patient: "Next Friday."

...

Doctor: "So, Mr. Brandberg, are you happy with your new hearing aid?"

Patient: "Very much, doctor. I already changed my last will twice!"

I feel like my body has gotten totally out of shape, so I got my doctor's permission to join a fitness club and start exercising…. I decided to take an aerobics class for seniors. I bent, twisted, gyrated, jumped up and down, and perspired for an hour. But, by the time I got my leotards on, the class was over.

. . .

Boy: "Wow, so many scars. You must have had an adventurous life!"

Old man: "No, I just have a cat."

. . .

A man said to a preacher, "That was an excellent sermon, but it was not original." The preacher was taken aback. The man said he had a book at home containing every word the preacher used. The next day the man brought the preacher a dictionary. Daily Phoenix, April 4, 1872.

SENIOR CITIZEN TEXTING CODES

ATD - At The Doctors

BFF - Best Friend Fell

BTW - Bring The Wheelchair

BYOT - Bring Your Own Teeth

FWIW - Forgot Where I Was

GGPBL - Gotta Go Pacemaker Battery Low

GHA - Got Heartburn Again

IMMO - Is My Hearing-Aid On

LMDO - Laughing My Dentures Out

OMMR - On My Message Recliner

OMSG - Oh My! Sorry, Gas

ROFLACGU - Rolling on Floor Laughing and Can't Get Up

TTYL - Talk to You Louder

REMEMBER

You don't stop laughing

because you grow old.

You grow old

because you stop

LAUGHING.

DON T FORGET TO LEAVE AN AMAZON REVIEW

We hope that you enjoyed reading every page of this book. *The Timeless Collection of Old Age Jokes* was created to make you laugh, improve your mood, relieve your stress, and have something to share with your family and friends. We hope you had fun laughing and sharing it with everyone!

See you at our next funny joke book!

OTHER BOOKS YOU MAY LIKE
SENIOR BRAIN WORKOUTS

Aging is inevitable, but brain fitness can be something that you can always be prepared. Never think twice, aging is bound to happen no matter how you avoid it. Train your brain as early as now.

SENIOR BRAIN WORKOUT BOOK 1:

Trivia for Seniors: 365 Fun and Exciting Questions and Riddles and That Will Test Your Memory, Challenge Your Thinking, And Keep Your Brain Young

Find it on Amazon at:

http://bit.ly/TriviaforSeniors

SENIOR BRAIN WORKOUT BOOK 2:

Trivia for Seniors: Keep Your Brain Young with 365 Exciting and Challenging Questions of Events from the 50s, 60s, 70s, and 80s!

Find it on Amazon at:
https://bit.ly/TriviaforSeniorsBook2

SENIOR BRAIN WORKOUT BOOK 3:

Trivia for Seniors: Random and Funny Edition.
365 Hilariously Random Questions That Will Test Your Wit, Develop Your Sense of Humor and Keep Your Brain Young

Find it on Amazon at:
https://bit.ly/TriviaforSeniorsBook3

SENIOR BRAIN WORKOUT BOOK 4:

Trivia for Seniors: All-American Edition. 365 Fun and Stimulating Questions That Will Challenge Your Memory, Test Your American History, And Keep Your Brain Young

Find it on Amazon at:
https://bit.ly/TriviaforSeniorsBook4

SENIOR BRAIN WORKOUT BOOK 5:

Bible Trivia for Seniors: A Fun, Brain-Boosting Question Game to Test Your Knowledge of Scripture, Strengthen Your Faith, and Keep Your Brain Young

Find it on Amazon at:
https://bit.ly/TriviaforSeniorsBook5

SENIOR FITNESS

Exercise is undeniably important- even more so for seniors. Exercises and weight training into old age has been proven to be one of the keys to longevity and vitality. Many seniors feel intimated by exercising because of the risks and pain associated with it. Let me tell you that, with the right guide, just about anyone can begin an exercise routine and improve their physique! In Senior Fitness, I try to do just that- provide you with a guide that will test your level of fitness and offer you tailored workout routines and customizable exercises that will adjust to your needs.

If you're ready to get fit and feel at least 10 years younger, then get your copy of Senior Fitness today!

Find it on Amazon at:

http://bit.ly/SeniorFitn

Made in the USA
Monee, IL
30 November 2022

18849320R00077